March 1981
Prestatyn

At the Edge of Town

At the Edge of Town

John Davies

Gomer Press,
Llandysul,
Dyfed.

First Impression - March 1981

ISBN 0 85088 923 5

Printed by J. D. Lewis and Sons Ltd.,
Gomer Press, Llandysul, Dyfed.

This book is published
with the assistance of the Welsh Arts Council.

For Betty and Vyrnwy

ACKNOWLEDGEMENTS

Some of the poems have been published in *Poetry Wales, The Anglo-Welsh Review, Phoenix, Use of English, Planet* and *Madog*. One was written for and used by the Welsh Arts Council 'Dial-a-Poem' service, others broadcast on BBC Radio 3 and Radio Wales, and another features on the long-playing EMI record 'Another Round of Poems and Pints'.

Some, too, were included in my pamphlet *Strangers* (Christopher Davies, 1974), and in the anthologies *Poems '73* (Gomer Press), *Green Horse* (Christopher Davies, 1978), *Andrew Young: Remembrance and Homage* (Tidal Press, Maine, U.S.A., 1978), and *Poems '78* (Gomer Press).

CONTENTS

PICTURE TIME

And here's a picture of Gareth's new girl at last,
eyes like bees emerging from a golden hive.
Black gloves; cigarette holder. We're aghast
with admiration, and "You next, boy!" we tell him,
shuffling the pack, fast-dealing him a wife.

Then someone's kids shine out like bells
ringing their laughter through that day beyond
to us. Persuaded by what innocence foretells,
we find "poor Arthur" next, embarrassing; silence
as, carefully, he's helped from hand to hand.

I like this picture of Marilyn beaming widely,
hair brimming from a wide-brimmed hat.
There are my parents. Janet. Dr. Tom. I see
people focused, pinned down almost by each clear
truth yet, without moving, swerving to evade it.

That was Hywel's wedding-day then, a golden fuss,
when the sun came out like a bold, cheerful man
raising his hat, and we waved, and all of us
made almost each of us quite sure, for once,
just what we were — ex-islands now become the main.

What's left for us are these much-fancied traces.
We sit here, all together now, watching them trot
between us, running again through their paces.
Between us, though, they are: reflections of ourselves
that could have frozen us in isolation, and did not.

13

THE FALLING

(for John Harries)

After-the-War, for some, became the after-war
That tricks with snags the brightest day.
And still some live on what they felt and saw,

The past groping, fumbling, near — a claw
To tear all that's present clumsily away
And leave them, from its passing, raw.

They know no longer what the struggle's for,
Last of the convoy-numbed, the jungle-grey.
Why this shaking at the day's soft core?

They, the distant not-quite-odd, abhor
The heat and prickle of the average day:
Icemen grown, they've forgotten how to thaw.

John, you neither sang your own lament nor
Flailed about to keep this truth at bay,
That for you what's past was unrelenting law.

After-the-War, for some, became the after-war.
It tricked with snags your brightest day.
It wore you down, it wore you clean away.

AFTER A WESTERN

I recognised that town
at the border, where silence
and stillness met in the one
street dusty as a fence.

In time, dust must have
settled on men's lives,
saddling them with habits,
souring the wives,

turning horizons into
a corral of red dust
and, at the last, change
into a change of dust.

Some, a few, left the town
to make their dreams a fact.
I recognised the ones who
stayed, keeping it intact,

each wondering perhaps if
he had really chosen to stay —
or whether staying had
chosen him, unmoving prey

for winds that brought
from the plain's grey crust
over cacti, through the heat,
promises and dust and dust.

FIRST SNOW

This whole new world
           of snow is boundless,
hard edges having softened
           in surprise so that
now things and people
           flow into roundedness,

the abandoned cars
           hunched, at rest, and houses
drowsily becoming homes.
           People are stirred out of
silence and themselves
           by what mystery arouses

and strangers greet each other;
           vaguely, we share a sense
of wandering in some
           foreign land — bemused,
content, happy now
           at meeting by coincidence.

I have seen men lean
           on shovels, done with talk,
standing where driveways
           were, to stare across
what might be roads
           at hills turned overnight to chalk.

So, for a time, we are
           slowed into simplicity,
bound together by this
           drift of more than snow.
Such joy, such joy if
           it could live on like the sea...

No, roundedness would
                surely revert to edges fast
as boredom came, then ice.
                The glory of whatever's new
and strange and shared
                is mainly that it cannot last.

DANDELIONS

Now, they are fleeing downstream, those dandelions
my small daughter has not-quite-thrown:
she raised her arm and let them go, and
the bridge sent its long dark shadow after them.

They flutter around boulders, wriggle, risk
the trees' fingers trailing, as though to justify
not just her casual faith in them but, too,
momentum, what the casually hurrying river's for.

She stands, beckoning at water and dandelions
and the sunlit afternoon. And I cannot tell her why,
now that she wants them back, they are beyond us
both. Useless to explain the river runs one way.

CERI

Laughter turned to tears
at the water's edge,
though we had played there
before. All your new fears

hurt: I jumped forward,
startled, to lift you
back from the quiet water,
almost caught off guard,

so now in my arms you ride
as waves unroll like carpets.
To you, I suppose,
they were a kind of landslide

falling from the horizon
in loud slow motion.
You are chatting again,
at ease, all tears gone.

And for you, for me,
as we drift back home,
I wish it was always
going to be this easy.

THE COMEBACK

"You the turn? Welcome to town,
squire. Interesting name: let's hope
the mike don't let you down."

> Makeshift stage. M.C. humbly lowing
> in a barnlike room half-empty.
> Then, at eight sharp, the Coming.

"Can't dance! Can't sing!": in front
three blokes sprawled out like kings.
"Must be a joke, mate — a Rag stunt!"

> Though the devil chills, warmth saves.
> Outside in the dark, gusts ride upon
> each other's backs in waves.

"Why didn't someone say? A sermon!
I'm off to check those bloody sheep —
then telly. 'Bye, all: must run."

> The voice which, voyaging the room,
> has sailed serenely on towards the
> port of Silence, docks quite soon.

"Seen worse. No, wasn't a bad draw,
not bad," a wise man wisely said.
"Can't beat Frankie Vaughan though."

> All over? Here's to the girl who alone
> thought he really was the Greatest
> and told him so and walked him home.

BARNS

Michigan; it is dusk.
We are driving
past big red barns with
farmhouses moored alongside
on a road so flat and
straight it ends in sky,
watching tides of trees
send darkness slowly in
through fences over the pale stubble
to flood the fields and road.
Fading, the barns are almost
all we have by now;
without them, anchored,
where would the horizon be?
It is good to be drifting
near depths of sleep, clear-eyed,
knowing someone else must be
out here where we have
never been before — but not
close enough to tell us so.
Our lights have just
stretched out ahead like arms
and we do not speak.
As the car points into darkness,
I am moving and not moving,
relaxed, unsure where I am,
at home but reaching
at last for what's new.
And since happiness
is a kind of balancing,
then the car and those barns
and the sunken fields
have made me happy now.

COUNTRY QUEST (1)

1.
Having shod his garage with lucky shoes,
made that concrete pond near which the gnomes
eye modest elves placed carefully in twos
and repaired the arch on which woodbine roams,
my neighbour's tending still his rustic dream.
Notice an old-new coach-lamp at his door —
no, his solid home's not what it might seem:
it is rooted in the street, the town, no more.

Not that I scorn his dream. Through webs of wire
on restless afternoons, I've glimpsed flash forth
a spark from sunlit summer leaves' green fire

then failed to catch the miracle in words.
Fulfilment, you could say, eludes us both:
the bird-bath in his garden tempts no birds.

2.
Near the beach, people watch the sea like spies,
from cars, and folk music is popular
in bungalows strewn like seed on this rise
once ploughed and tilled where now commuters are.
Oak Street, The Meadows, and Laburnum Row
yawn at each other's lies and doze, packed tight.
Where horizons beckoned, silvery aerials glow;
television blots out the sky at night.

Slowly we've trekked away from and not towards;
wrapped in luxuries against surprise,
we've built out of our senses' withered cords
walls against what we've lost and yet still prize.
Drowsing here now, in the car's bright hearse
and at home, is the Frontier in reverse.

22

3.

Along the lane, green blur of hedges; then the hill.
We came down again on roofs warming in sunlight
around a glistening steeple, and left the car
and walked — on our need's pilgrimage still.

Faces in half-open windows seemed to promise us
the river's secret, murmured from its bed of stone;
elm-trees drowsily tussled with the heat;
somewhere, chickens made their muffled farmyard fuss.

After winters in town we return each summer now,
though less often, believing meanwhile that summer's
always there, that shadowless hearts and days exist.
Each time, we're more eager to fulfil the vow

we'd find a place at last where dreams might happen.
The water's secret though, those people seem to share...
sometimes, cold as unease, the same rain as elsewhere
blurs faces that we see. We return home then.

23

ANOTHER LEGEND

A stranger stopped to give two girls a lift,
said " 'Scuse me just a sec,'' and swift

-ly vaulted like a dream the wall
which met the crumbling mountainfall

apparently. Girls waited. Smoked. Didn't shout
but made for Conway. Too cool to hang about.

Those who *must* leap when girls are around
should check they'll land upon firm ground,

red blood being what it is — and life's ravines
so often graveyards not latrines.

DOWNSTAIRS

Coming like that down the dark stairs
to feel, in the sudden switched-on room,
that something had just left as if
a-scurry from light's excited bloom,
was to catch (gaping and unawares
for a second, for once) life's other life.

The black window betrayed everything
nearly: the chair's soft moss; that loam
of carpet, shadows growing. Too late,
my cough was like a bolt pushed home
against the night and what nights bring
to the heart of things apparently well-lit.

Then to move forward, press a switch,
bring music sprinting from the radio,
was to pretend not just new morning
but that there was, after all, no more
to be asserted — not a home, toys
clinging to a corner, not work calling.

Bed was another place, the dark a blanket
round our breathing. Beyond, just rain.
Our daughter stirred nearby. And I know
that although what's gone will come again
sometime and still not be seen, yet
what we have will be my Yes against its no.
It will come; I'll speak. And it will go.

A HAPPENING

It was Mayor Sunlight performed
the ceremony: glowing, he unveiled
Snowdonia snowbound in the sky,

an empire in fierce white flames
as an hour's proof forever
of what is possible in Spring.

Then it was gone; Mayor Sunlight
bowed proudly and went out.
All the people were amazed.

FOR MR. DYAS

Your wife dead now, you old
and blind, it seems to me
you carry aloft the last flag
of a ruined city under siege,
your sightless eyes outstaring all
that is against you, hearing others
depart, but going on without complaint,
your speech laid firmly down like
a gauntlet for whatever general
stuck you in an outpost in the dark,
your voice a torch in our own small
dark, and that upright walk an advance
into symbol, you having now become
your flag, I a witness not of what
you stood for but for how long
through what assaults you stood —
and of how you stood.
        And how you stood.

SUNNY PRESTATYN

Each day I see them carefully grow old and feed
      behind that glass, those plants,
in an aquarium's stillness — saw at first their need
      for aloneness like a niche.
It is not a need. Lured by some sun-crossed memory
      of August, most have retired
from industrial towns at last to find the sea
      sucked out of reach.

They have left the wet streets that flow
      on Northern towns like tides,
those separately secret worlds that tow
      forever in their wake
lives bound by the going and returning they inhabit,
      for this quiet place
where silent mornings on the daylight hours sit.
      Here no tide will break.

Some watch the sand, the blank sea stretching out, going
      endlessly nowhere.
Past bungalows, an empty paper bag goes yachting
      down the empty street.
Cars pass; seagulls stream on white safaris to the sea.
      Like their bungalows,
the old here are detached, with no shared memory
      to sift or curse or greet.

And if they had known of this, would they have stayed
        where home and friends
still were, where the family once was, and made
        the most of their discharge?
Anywhere, lack of interest, change and age itself condemn
        them, left on some beach
or trapped in tanks. We are accused of them
        and they are us writ large.

AT THE ZOO

I've never been too keen on lions and
tigers, those decision-makers, frankly.
From my leafy covert here, all that
bunched exhibitionist-machismo just
to show off the quickest route from A to B
seems excessive. Why waste energy?

Elephants again: too many of them have
leant on me. Large-bottomed in middle age,
huge jowled but small of eye, they will
keep trumpeting as if I'm drunk or simple.
So I perch there, dull as an empty page,
eyes blank, too numb to be enraged.

I much prefer small things half-visible
and quiet (I don't know half their names)
that squirrel at the back of littered rooms,
doing interesting, shy things with straw.
Their lives seem to be an enigmatic game.
Trivial, I know. I like them just the same.

The boring task, that wastes our time, of
proving things to folk in next door's cage
doesn't seem to interest them at all —
they've opted out, signed off. So I watch
with quiet respect each quietly busy sage
twiddling, not tearing, towards old age.

TWO PEOPLE IN A GARAGE

They were roosting comfortably at their garage door
in round armchairs like nests, watching rain
turn all the bungalows opposite to dripping cardboard.
Baffled, I stared, hurried on — then slowed again.

It was afternoon; windows examined us impassively
as the woman, giggling, nudged her husband.
"We fell out!" he yelled, and at once I saw the picture
clearly: their bungalow tilting up as though on sand,

doors banging, cupboards gaping with surprise or joy
and pictures hanging at mad angles, trophies riding
triumphantly at last from shadowy cabinets, the chairs
and television set on skates, and those two sliding

helplessly content in two armchairs straight into
that garage nearby to hear their laughter roam.
Drowsily, they settled back to gaze. I waved.
And a trace of sunlight marked the short path home.

VISIT

An old knife-grinder called, seemed keen to talk.
I fobbed him off with knives which, sharp already,
could have scalped a tree, and later a cork
popped from our garage where he worked. Unsteady,
wiping a hand across his mouth, he asked
for something warm. So a mug of tea I laid
on the garage floor and quickly left — then basked
in the shadow, after, of the note I paid.

"Better watch your friend!" a neighbour said
(his shed was locked up like a fort, I saw),
and out of double-barrelled eyes smiled lead.
Leaving, the old man talked about the War,
started mumbling about the cold; it was late.
We watched him till he'd passed the gate.

DUSK

light from
the slow dying
day leaked through
evening leeches of it
dark yellow swelling in
trees around pale leaves
to seal off all the sky
with something more than
air and bear down from
nothingness onto the
softly   collapsing
husk of nowhere
starting me
moving
moving
almost clear
away again from
knowing that the
source of such light
isn't merely a sun nor
just the heart but that
like sand sliding silent
always from one globe to
the other gathering more
yellowness it must fill
in time the whole
the whole of my
being still

LESSONS

Some days we are on a country railway, halted.
For hours, seemingly, my every class
cut off in what the fields pretend is silence,
I can feel our day relax on either side like
platforms grown too much at one with grass,
and too at ease, for quiescence to be faulted.

Or we're an airport sometimes. Through noise
takes off expectant self-absorption bound
for glory somewhere else; there's a quickening,
a surge of coming-from and going-to, the room
a hall of glass beyond me. Then, I am the sound
of the muffled tannoy chanting of my voice.

But most often we are here, in kinds of parity
between extremes. In search of a middle way,
I watch the children ripple through gradual
ebbings, swells. And I think the best times come
when work, dressed-up in odds and ends for play
but serious, is like a charade before a party.

Here, content to let my being almost still
define what movement is, and change, I share
a sense of journeying with those in flux
who flow, break flustering on stones, and flow
again through a river's turbulence of air
or who, floating, nonchalantly ease downhill.

I am changed by them. A portion of the banks,
growing more and less myself as waters reel
or saunter by, I am altered by them.
And I take the lessening with the increase:
when its banks accommodate a river, I feel
the river's renewal of them is in lieu of thanks.

FOR ANDREW YOUNG

In a high green pool overhead
that August afternoon, leaves
on the surface, drowsing, slow
-ly rearranged themselves; they turned
to rest again, lolling on reefs of shadow.

I stared up through shallows like
pale lawns into the drowned greengage
orchards. And, deepening behind,
green was ripening gradually to darkness,
towing the gaze, the heart, beyond the mind.

Sometimes the water dazzle shone right
down. It blessed the lane. I trod — I was
water. You knew such water's never
far. Is around us always and (you said, precise
about the mystery) beyond us all for ever.

HOW TO WRITE
ANGLO-WELSH POETRY

It's not too late, I suppose...
You could sound a Last Post or two,
and if you can get away with saying
what's been said, then do.

First, apologise for not being able
to speak Welsh. Go on: apologise.
Being Anglo-*any*thing is really tough;
any gaps you can fill with sighs.

And get some roots, juggle names like
Taliesin and ap Gwilym, weave
A Cymric web. It doesn't matter what
they wrote. Look, let's not be naive.

Now you can go on about the past
being more real than the present —
you've read your early R. S. Thomas,
you know where Welsh Wales went.

Spray place-names around. Caernarfon.
Cwmtwrch. Have, perhaps, a Swansea
sun marooned in Glamorgan's troubled
skies; even the weather's Welsh, see.

But a mining town is best, of course,
for impact, and you'll know what to say
about Valley Characters, the heart's dust
and the rest. Read it all up anyway.

A quick reference to cynghanedd
always goes down well; girls are cariad;
myth is in; exile, defeat, hills ...
almost anything Welsh and sad.

Style now. Nothing fancy: write
all your messages as prose then chop
them up — it's how deeply red and green
they bleed that counts. Right, stop.

That's it, you've finished for now —
just brush the poems down: dead, fluffed
things but your own almost. Get
them mounted in magazines. Or stuffed.

LETTER TO A COMEDIAN
(for Tony Hancock)

Dear Sir,
> I have watched you
> as years washed past
>
> reflect those
> depths you dragged
> for laughter to the last.
>
> It seemed to me
> at times you were
> drowning fast —
>
> not frantically
> flailing but
> your eyes aghast.
>
> Now, surfacing again,
> your smile drips effort
> and you grin for air.
>
> I should like
> to say at last
> (the horizon's bare)
>
> that all of this
> is mine, this
> sea we share.
>
>> I am
>> yours faithfully,
>> Despair.

ANOTHER KIND

Fallen leaves in mould
    I've watched a soundless
autumn's alchemy make gold

        and sensed, as night began to lap
          the leaves, an old
        disquiet sprung like a trap.

Dusk too — I've seen its name
    burn through a fragile map
of sky in streaks of flame.

        Then, unaware, I have veered beyond
          the path into that same
        sprung trap, light's broken bond.

Light is its own requiem. To wear
    night's cloak when its wand
has turned thought into a snare

        needs a faith's enduring brightness —
          or dreams brushed on air,
        another kind of starriness.

In the dark, I can make occasionally
    a landscape much less
durable than faith, a country

        crossed by streams of pale light
          where no shadows are, briefly
        glimpsed but forever clear of night,

which leaves me, when it fades far
    into the present out of sight,
a small sufficient brightness like a star.

ON THE BEACH

My child's toy motor boat
is an oil-breaker now,
keel-deep in pools of froth
while nearby waves collapse
like low brick walls.

We watch tankers pretend to move
on Liverpool: the sea invites
and they come so quietly;
flattened on the grey
horizon's wall.

In summer, while untanned tourists
clamber from the sea light brown
and gambol and return for more,
the locals on the promenade
pause now and then to stare

like an older generation
watching their children scramble
on a building-site, who, not having
grown attached to grass,
now gaily make the best of brick.

IN MICHIGAN

near the broccoli-phoenix
rising from green ashes
Eddie

        mad at his wife's
        mouth on cheeks perched
        cheeping

straightens to
land spadefuls
thrashed and beached

        his two children's
        worm-crazy beaks
        forgotten

and pisses a straight line
to set things a-growing
("Beans that'll riot!")

        as the other job
        vainly beats white wings
        against his collar

riffles some earth
like it was dollar bills
and whistles

        (laying down wire
        netting on what
        he loves the most)

and murmurs, not to me,
"We may be ugly but
we got the music, man".

HEROES

Things that we cannot do and do not say
surround us like walls we come to accept
apparently; pacing between them this way
doesn't seem to bruise us ever — except

sometimes, perhaps, measuring their height
while light's frail ladder under the window
fades and another sun skates out of sight,
and when later the lamp inside's turned low.

Which is why, I suppose, we discard each
hero in the end: too big for a cell,
he makes ours seem well out of living's reach.

We admire, before our rooms clench one by one,
but then "He's us, after all!" we must yell.
And grin at him medals for presumption.

FOR A STAR

Luminous, a star,
was what you wished to be,
even when directed
to that loneliness of sky.

Such a glitter was
demanded at that height
you trembled, wondered
where you ended
and your style began, or if style
had banished self so utterly
you merely lived to shine.

You were watched forever.
Husbands could not change
your role, nor — till the end —
those tablets your despair.

Down to your long, last
lying on a pillow,
perfect blondeness now
no longer a reproach
to our starved lives
or your star-silvered
starlessness, you were
what we wanted you to be.

GELERT

We bought a little person
after being married awhile
to fill the space between us
with a yard of doggy fun,

and when he drooled at us
we knew it must be love:
we three smiled so often together
he became love's buttress

and our conversation-piece combined.
Guests said that, yes, they loved
his trick of panting hoarsely; they
praised us for his singing when he pined.

If he barked at cats and frogs,
of course, we taught him discipline
and once I dreamt contentedly
of Nuremburg, of being hailed by dogs . . .

Also, we taught him to endure
being caged all day
till eventually his tiresome
bursts of life grew fewer.

So he became stoical like us,
and fat, and when he died
(run over by our vacuum cleaner)
we didn't make a fuss.

We were worthy of him maybe.
We leashed ourselves again
to silence for a decent interval
then had a baby.

SEPTEMBER WIND

We heard a wind
break suddenly into the gardens,
strum stalks
and rattle hedges.
Startled, leaves
scattered or from
dim retreats were torn.
The flowers stood aside,
brittle children,
their heads shorn.

You stared and turned,
then raptly watched again
that force reap
over-ripeness in a storm
of leaves and petals.
Distanced it was, but
how much more than glass away?
Were you compliant or
envious perhaps?
Or carefully at bay?

WATERS

1   The afternoon, suspended until then
by light's pale strands on a wall of sky,
had turned to dusk. I stood near that canal
watching my shadowy reflection fail to untie
itself from the stillness it had chosen,

and thought of water slumping into locks:
a canal doesn't scramble to the sea,
change course or carve and gouge its name
in rock till the name becomes a valley.
It is water growing old within a box.

Ahead, the canal stretched into twilight
as a haze of greys and greenness someone
would always need to measure stillness by,
where water's silent ease in its restriction
denied that water ever hungered to be white.

Then dusk was going, dwindling like a dream.
Trees stirred; I heard the wind's first shiver
shake the grass, but stayed watching water
still refuse to stir. Somewhere, a river
fanatically onward ran — a river or a stream.

2   I saw a man lean on a bridge and gaze
into a drumming stream I could not see
as though, swollen by its weight of leaden days,
water had unloosed for him a flurry
of reeds like memories into its maze
and so brought gradually downstream maybe,
to that perfect centre of all his ways,
those which had floated most tenaciously.

Perhaps he was blind to strands the water towed.
But his unchanging, rapt absorption still
in what through or underneath him flowed
meant that for me, too, beyond power of will,
where I was going mattered then much less
than that flux, our reason for unhurriedness.

3   Hurrying from work like
    other traffic, I was crossing
    the Huron bridge again,
    the river ambling at ease
    in a course it had made itself,

    when two middle-aged black
    women in coats went by
    with fishing-rods and folded
    chairs. They were laughing about
    things beyond me then, and now.

    I know the river is not just
    to be crossed, have glimpsed what
    it makes of shadows and stones
    and sunlight running from me
    under overhanging branches.

    It's meant mainly though, I think,
    for middle-aged black women
    who can turn to it on bright cold
    days as naturally as falling asleep
    to find what bridges never reach.

AT THE POLONA

'A double room at the Polona
looking out to sea';

I've tried making room for you,
and you for me.

Alone, we have doubled our silence
so successfully

now we can't unpack what we'd like
perhaps to see:

silence leaves too little room
for you and me.

A fresh start? Again? We've doubled
back repeatedly.

There is no room for both of us.
We are looking out to sea.

CURTAINS

September offered us white feathers
adrift on that cricket field
we circled; rising, the breeze
ran on ahead to begin dismantling
billowing big tops of trees.

And November one day. Flakes of rain
on the pond again and on our talking,
water dimpling water, as around we went,
trembling its marshy edges, going
not far — no further than we'd meant.

Deep in her room once, your aunt said,
"Something is moving under the Christmas
tree," and you smiled. But silent there,
I heard the letter-box chatter.
Curtains were hanging like hair.

Now, I recognise that essential single
room where we sat in growing darkness,
dwindling and growing shadowy
in a space less shared than
sub-let to one another briefly.

Around no spreading chestnut tree,
I sought you as you sought me.
And voices, never quite clear enough,
live just on air for a single moment
when the radio is switched off.

WHERE WE ARE NOW

Straying when young, I'd glimpse Love Lane,
its green fullness fading into shadow
into greenness gradually again —

a whole round world seemed wrapped
warm-furled there like a fern upon itself
in a silence fields and that river lapped.

Now, tracking the dream's green source
disturbs the dream: like summer,
silence is taken endlessly by force,

by winds and voices blasting its surprise.
What world's complete, unalterably whole?
Not, as this humming summer flies,

this wholeness you and I have found.
Listen to the leaves though. That one bird.
For now, they drown all other sound.

CAT COUNTRY

At the town's edge: land
like a cat reverting
to almost-jungle
in undergrowth where sand

sifts purring, a tawny
shadowness under grass
and brown fern curled.
Nearby, the dunes and sea.

It has scratched down
fences, lapped its stream
to mud as it prowls the
frontier of the town.

And survives its lair:
at bay, it has out-
grown all the poison
we have dumped there.

Near streets, crouched taut
along a path, this land
is both hunter stalking
and hunted almost caught

as we've moved on it
wall by wall, cars revving
nearer, its nights by
sudden headlamps slit.

DAYS WHEN THERE WAS MIST

Mist brought in the horizon like a trawl
across the fields, netting pylons and then
sheep floating, the hedges all distant land.
At midday it was already dusk. The mist
drifted over and beneath and through me
gradually like a sleep in which, fading,
I was just a shape dreamt by mist.

Later, dry winds blew the horizon back.
A track of sorts began planning vaguely
where I had to go. As I headed towards
cluttered islands of bright roofs,
awake, I thought about other mists
that tempt, delight, deceive, before
the mist that goes on and on without end.

Just to the Left,
ladies and gentlemen,
see all that sea-mist lie
around a marvellous mountain
promising the sky.

The peak seems as
accessible as the moon
above a hedge; white
paths to the summit
glitter and invite.

Notice their narrowness
though, that mist,
huge rocks in the fern
like littered errors.
The boat will now return.

Mist seemed to rub the house most of that day
smudging with weightless hands each window-pane
and all childhood's country, a haze away.
Glad to be at home together again,
we traced shared references on fragile maps
sketched first where that country's frontier lies
and revised, re-sketched, mislaid perhaps —
returning then, they took us by surprise.
We'd mapped the country each to different scales,
as now, mist fingering the roads and hill;
what greyness finally rubs out or veils
for ever, though, united us all still.
I glanced out: mist, persistent as the grass,
was binding our reflections in the glass.

UP HERE

Down in easy country, towns and villages seem
flat stages on the way to somewhere else
as if holding out, just waiting to be called at last
to an unnamed rainbow city where the road ends.
Some coastal towns, for instance, look like
admiring spectators. Strung along burnished roads,
identically dressed in garages, hotels and cafes,
they're poised on the verge of going home apparently.

It's different high in the bouldered hills:
this village seems content to be here. Having had
to accommodate itself to curved uniqueness,
it has remained itself distinctly, still
changing now, in woven light and shadow dressed.
So roads through the narrow passes trickle in —
no reaching out for miles to the rainbowed Somewhere
that, dissolving mistily, is always somewhere else.

A PARTY IN DETROIT
(Dec., 1974)

I think the Professor
has made this speech about
Nixon and Vietgate before.
His finger drills my chest.

He insists he is irish
(he has not been home
in almost thirty years)
and therefore disengaged —

like the girl I know
who said that, travelling
through France last year,
she'd called herself canadian.

There is not much talk
about being American...
everyone is german-irish,
Black, italian-polish now.

At times, the Golden Gate
itself must dream uneasily
of people slumped in Oldsmobiles
heading vaguely for the sea

from areas of themselves
like empty houses, the chairs
still nodding on verandahs,
and copies of LIFE magazine

with Kennedy pictures
strewn over gaping floors,
toy guns on some of the lawns.
The Professor has already left.

COUNTRY QUEST (2)

The Clwyd coast, you say, is a caravan
with window-stickers (Prestatyn, Sunny Rhyl)
brought piece by piece on the autobahn
that threads industrial Europe then uphill
through Wales by Midland Holiday Holdings Inc.
I listen: the familiar homily.
It'll soon be everywhere, you think,
a kind of veneered life-facsimile,
for the countryside's growing less itself,
more part of the main. And when at last,
the story goes, what's old is on the shelf
or lost, we'll find ourselves stuck fast
to packages we've taken in unseen.
From nowhere land they'll be, all icy clean.

Well, I'm tired of the old nostalgia game.
The cottages stuffed with home-made bread
or bards; fields of corn, and poems the same,
in endless summer like a feather bed...
I can do without them all for a bit.
Pastoral innocence, that sacred cow,
has bred a car-sick urban linnet.
Caradoc Evans, thou shouldst be living now.
We are going to have to take what's here
to stay, make less of that tempting blur,
our dream-past. And to accept what is new
as something most have travelled to —
as when, rumbustious March having died,
the doors of caravans in Spring fling wide.

PORT TALBOT

The breakers' jumbled yard: valley,
hills, strewn plain, reflect back
undulations of the sea.

Where steel and tidal water meet,
not turbulence and steam
but rust, what's left of heat,

is breaking down crisp ore
almost to the heart, the heart's
still beating core.

Mist's rolling-mills in sheets
send rain. There's sun. But night
alone here alters what it meets —

even when, silent, a furnace-flare
will flatter all the sleeping sky
like a dream of what was here,

three glimmering decades outstared
now by a ghost — and only
rust is eager and red-haired

in no-man's land, this town,
my town, whose thunder's the sound
of thunder running down.

MAX BOYCE

Warm blurred noise at the clubface;
a previous act leaves for the Bridge.
And then unfrosted mirrors in your humour,
glinting, remind us where we still belong
and why our laughter's echoed over
Wales. At ease together, bound for once
by more than just accent, rumour,
traces on a map, we share your song
and ourselves in this warm place.

Outside, the landscape will be stark —
and it's not your fault if hymns
to rugby, adrift there in a world of frost
above book-haunted Institutes, deft
bingo-chapels, all those moonlit
dreaming graves of socialism and faith,
measure mainly what's been lost.
You harvest something of what's left
as you lead this singing in the dark.

FOUND POEM

"I know all about the Arabs,"
said nanny Gronstein

from Port Talbot, who is
an Argon welder by trade.

"They come over for Ramadan
to Port Talbot to miss it

in their own country. They
pray on mats, don't they?"

(from *The Guardian*)

GLIMPSES OF MISS PRIOR

1   Under a private sky across the street
is where Miss Prior sleeps
in a quiet room in that secret house
through which the moonlight seeps.

I think I almost see at times
what shadows cross her lawn,
waiting until she'd done with sleep
to revisit her at dawn,

to sit with her through fragile days
and, going, leave no traces.
Her cat walks through a dream of legs;
her silences have faces.

2   Hearing Miss Prior opposite
address her cat amused me
once — that electronic
organ too, warbling at night.
We've met since then.
She seems to keep herself
for a long-awaited guest
whose face she would not recognise
now or remember why she waited,
sending out most nights
from her rainwashed pier
tunes that reach jauntily
for deck-chairs and the sand
under silences postponed
but not forgotten,
voracious and inevitable,
waiting overhead like gulls.

3   Ageing with grace,
    she offers me
    a pride of photographs:
    still-lives more
    lifeless still
    the more she insists
    she too has known
    the dawn break
    shining white on black.

    I see them all
    except one she palms.
    A ghost perhaps, smiling,
    summoning her back?
    Sifting what's past
    disturbs us, clarifies
    blurred fears that
    dawns come gradually
    a staler yellow on black.

4   I have sensed her turn
    gently to shadows,
    too wary of spaces
    to be caught long
    in openness —

    startled, the hart
    fades gradually into
    a kind of haze, away
    from what only
    the heart can guess.

By now, watching cool
eyes, she has learnt
to smile in lieu of saying,
is wary of what
others will seek

and so, lest uncovered
tracks uncover her,
she makes her deep woods
more deeply hers through
words she does not speak.

NEXT DOOR

He's there but, mole-like,
has burrowed out of sight.
People knock, depart; he is
almost silent — but not quite:

I hear him fumble nameless
tunes from a piano quietly
and, some nights, rustlings
behind my silence halt me.

Once, I dreamt he came soft
-footed, dusk upon his brow;
piano wire shone in his hands.
Doctor Death I call him now.

SMALL TOWNS

Part of me tonight
is with small towns in Alabama:
those shacks on the fringes leaning in wait
against trees for reasons to be upright,
and mobile homes with nowhere else to go,
then the frayed main streets, houses around
squares haunted by Civil War cannon and
each verandah's darkgreen velvet shadow,
by voices I half-believed were there.

Detached, apart from me
at times, were towns in Alabama.
As I travelled through Selma past blocks
of wooden slums towards Montgomery,
I stopped to eat at a small Black cafe
by mistake. There was a jail with black
faces, a racoon skin hanging from a branch.
More than the sun had drained not just the day
and Wallace country was a shrivelled lake.

I can think, though, of a part for me
in some small town in Alabama.
It requires me to sit upon a chair
a friend has made; the house has gradually
come to fit me, and my neighbours I know well.
There's dialogue, no change of scene. Little
happens, except I'll feel at home perhaps...
unless rootedness becomes a cell,
unlocked door tight shut, the window clouded.

For I am more than partly
small places anywhere
as I head towards them or away, sensing
in each that elusive, vague confederacy —
lines meeting in an almost open palm
(the childhood valleys of belonging
haunt me still) — afraid always of finding
in the end, after moving in, a settled calm
like a worked-out, recently abandoned farm.

TRAVELLING

Caught between fences on the road, wind
threshed the hedges, winnowing swirls of birds;
it shrilled and hummed telegraphs downwire,
made a hoarding stiffly drum its sides and
stamp. The locked trees trembled their unease.

I leant, winded, on a gate to watch openness
pour from the hillside over someone's fields
and saw fleet light flickerings of grass
flared green in the wind's escape and flashing
stopped, snuffed at my feet by the strung fence.

Wind tugged me; the way others had trodden out
and even then were treading, had lumbered
inevitably up to that unopened gate and
now, as clouds unfurled, it steered ahead
to the end of weather, a never-changing sky —

strange how, after stumbling aboard, we name Decision
stumbling's full momentum, the road progressing
so resolutely on towards where it has to go
that, often, trying to be apart from it,
we feel it happen underneath us as we drowse,

patiently turning back again later to point us
like children at what's too visible between rich,
vague feasts of land we have hardly known at all
which, though they came at the beginning perhaps,
do not come now, do not come to us when we call.

EPITAPH ON A CONVERSATION

The truth, green glimmer
of the light through leaves,
may be better gleaned
from other than the rustling
as a spry wind spins the trees:

from a glance perhaps,
or else from silence
as a hedgerow's sudden
clenching on itself
freezes a sunlit lane.

I think I know this bland,
wry wind I've just heard breathe
tall stories in the leaves —
it's the wind that
taught the willows weeping.

HORROR FILM

Of course the label's fang-in-cheek: the whirr
of vampires, those howls, are less horrific than there
to help us all forget we're so indubitably here.
Compared with this freaked-up nightmare,

Psycho was a documentary: Perkins twitching like a rat,
an old woman's voice and a shower and some stairs...
it definitely worried me, that.
What's familiar has the cosiest, nastiest snares.

A true horror film could show the castle as a street
and blood as nerves. The maiden trapped in darkness
really lives next door (sometimes you meet),
finds habit, that grisly mirror, comfortless

but always has the radio loud, and her eyes
howl into hours that slowly, separately leak
towards twilight when her husband comes. She'll rise;
soon he goes out; they never seem to speak.

And you, the bright hero, reminded of your own
four walls, don't even wave. In place of the madman
made out of wax, time broods. The Unknown is known —
the happy ending is you forget that, when you can.

THAT TENNIS COURT

I stumbled on
today too late,
at the far end
of the park.
The grass was
trodden down
the net slack
and through air
still warm from
recent use
rhododendron
bushes pushed
over thin white
lines a darkness
and an ending.
Soon it would cover
everything, I knew.
There were voices
but far off.

IN DECEMBER

1.

Something has strewn overhead
        blue sea then scattered
icebergs there for clouds and
        sprayed white sunlight on us
restlessly afloat surprised
        by water upside down
a christmas in midsummer
        and all our spaces are awash
with air so sharp it stiffens
        the rigging of our hair
in an age of sun and near
        silence as we sail, lone
craft that celebrate reunion in mid-voyage.

2.

    The impulse of
    the butterfly that
    fluttered out its time
    inside my window
    in December,

               the impulse for
               these words that
               fritter out their time
               on my sheet of paper
               in December,

    is a gift of air
    that, passing, lightly
    promising to keep
    fragility afloat, does
    not remember

most things die:
a poem tempted into
print, a butterfly
enticed to a garden
like an ember.
But butterfly
and poem now live here
awhile — if what sustained
the butterfly lets poems
outlast December.

FOR MARILYN

The joy that floating is, on air,
the sense of being everywhere,

the secret of this drifting high
into an endlessness of sky,

is the fixed point from and going to,
the being homeward-bound to you.